INSIGHT PUBLICA®

INSIGHT PUBLICA®
Nadakkave, Kozhikode, Kerala, India
www.insightpublica.com
e-mail: insightpublica@gmail.com

White Songs

Arun & Sunitha

(English Poems)

First Edition: November 2021

ISBN 978-93-5517-096-5
Printed and Published by
InsightinPublica Printers & Publishers Pvt Ltd.

WHITE SONGS

Arun & Sunitha

INSIGHT PUBLICA

Translator and artist, **Arunlal K** is widely published in both Malayalam and English. Apart from the several published national, international papers, academic books and poetry collections he has contributed to the research in International Shakespearean Desk, Dublin, Ireland. He currently works as Assistant Professor at the Dept. of English, Govt. College Mokeri.

Sunitha Srinivas.C has numerous national and international publications to her credit. She has also contributed extensively to journals of repute. A recipient of UGC fellowships, she is the author of academic books and poetry collections. She currently works as Associate Professor at the Dept. of English, Govt. College Mokeri.

PREFACE

"A poem is nothing. By persistence the poem can be made something; but then it's something, not a poem."

"What is a Poem?"
Laura Riding (Anarchism is Not Enough)

Authorship has been one of the most contested areas in the history of literary theory— the prevalent idea of authorship being that of an 'inspired genius' (who 'straddles the boundaries between man and God') creating works of art in isolation. A creative work was mostly seen as a reflection of the unitary author; of a 'solitary genius' (Stillinger). It was epitomized, among others, by the likes of P.B. Shelley who identified the Poet with a nightingale sitting in the darkness, singing in solitude. The paradigms of authorship thus mostly categorized a literary text as the expression of an author's 'hypertrophic self'. The triad of author-text-reader has been put under the scanner in many modes, and in many phases. There has been serious individualisation of the author-figure, contestation about whether the authorial figure determines meaning, whether the agency of the author is alive or dead; and there also appeared thoughts regarding virtual authorship in discussions about the works of cyber authors. Regardless of the theoretical dismissal of authorial intentions, the function of the author in being a helpful category to identify the text has thrived. Even beyond the book market, contemporarily, the author denotes more than merely a 'category.' As an individual, the author's biography is sought and attached with the book. This often determines the psychoanalytical deductions regarding the content of the book, the reach of the book to an international reading community, the identity politics along which the book's relevance is to be understood and so on. In this respect, the author for literature is an individual whose 'personality' is at least a componential presence in the whole act of reading and interpretation. In fact, to be able to write literature in the present context is an exceedingly individual act.

Contemporary common sense does not allow much space for combined authorships and related discourses. We now know how Shakespeare (like later Romantic writers) had collaborated with other writers while he wrote his plays. But increasingly we tend to pin the oeuvre on Shakespeare because we would like the author to be one person. Combined authorship or dispersed authorship is something that swims against the current, especially so in the case of poetry. Since the nineteenth century at the least, poetry has been the literary output of a single person. At the very beginning of *Lyrical Ballads*, Wordsworth announced that the business of poetry is all about an individual with a comprehensive soul and an observing eye—"The observing eye cannot be still: we cannot bid it so" he says. Poetry is an art that should hold the description of one person's vision of the world. The poet is an individual observer who tries to "get something right in language" (to use Howard Nemerov's phrase). The poet not only remains faithful to the contingencies of his or her heart but also adheres to the strict reality of the 'things' of the world. Writing recreates a person's way of understanding the world; the act of poeticizing the world both reproduces a visible external provocation and adds a new item to the totality of available reality. Writing together allows for the inclusion of multiple perspectives and voices. Collaborative creativity prods writing differently; every poem a performative event. Contrary to images of the lone, solitary writer, co-authorship (with a shared creative authority) poses a challenge to entrenched power dynamics. How can a single text possibly "manifest the essential being of more than one person"? As to this question, the reader will only be left guessing at the respective shares of the associated authors (the collaboration becoming the focus of creativity); for the authorial role is not in the hands of a single person, but is shared.

This book is our second attempt at combined authorship poetry, following *Orange Madrigals* which came out in 2014. Letting another author work through poems that one considers finished and well-made carries a spiritual risk. There is every possibility of losing both the poem and the friend. Poetry can be and in some respects ought to be more than individualistic (and we are not talking about editing and proofreading). In a larger sense it is discursive. Its idiom contains a need for the best possible communication. Even when it is meditative and philosophical, poetry anticipates participation. One is familiar with the way poetry has evolved post-millennia: social engagement, sexuality, and an overtly political agenda leaning on identity demands that it be plural and general. Poets have come to give us the description of the external world as they perceive it through the dispersal angle of their personality. They are not really autobiographical or confessional in general, in the traditional sense. Poems have become often anecdotal, though seldom confessional. There are larger moral, ethical, or aesthetic observations made by the individual.

Anecdote, fantasy and artefact inform the poems of this collection. Confessions and autobiographical vignettes do not make many appearances. Where the latter appears, they lose their specificities at the source since there is a second personality overwriting. Even when the overwriting leaves the original script as it is, it is still a secondly written work. It was allowed away by the creative mind that it be overridden by the other author. In the preface to the first collection, we did talk about the androgynous spirit and the gender split in literary imagination. Taking that thought further, in this collection we have put together visions of the androgynous and the other. The scope of this vision extends to the numinous. The poems move through a range of subjects and in a variety of tones. Although each has worked to develop a "style" or several styles apposite to the matters at hand, the main focus throughout these poems is on perfecting their methods of observation. In other words, we are concerned equally with styles of writing and writing itself as style. The Kantian theory that the realm of the "aesthetic" is an antidote to those trends in contemporary literary criticism that examine art through one of several political, sociological, or ideological lenses also need to be evoked in the context of this collection whose existence is primarily justified by its obsession with constructing an aesthetically different set of poems. Aesthetics, although never innocent of motive and never "pure," or lacking meaning and feeling, might prove a difficult measure of art's seriousness, as we often confuse it as 'simple' ornament. How do a varied aesthetics convey meaning in a different way? What is the difference when two authors describe something? Won't the "I" interfere with, interrupt, and influence the seeing "eye"? As Marjorie Hope Nicholson said in the context of answering a question pertaining to the composing of a poem: "(D)escription is not that artificial thing—a 'form of discourse'; it is the use of several moods or attitudes of mind through which a writer or speaker, who has found his world interesting, beautiful, ugly, or effective, endeavours to transfer to others his pleasure or his interest in that world." Words for the sake of poetic beauty ought to be reintroduced into literature. In writing aesthetically pleasing poetry, one is not choosing a neutral position: it always carries the freight of an unannounced purpose, a politics that is beyond the contemporary frames of realpolitik. Poetry that is collected here, we suppose, is marked by that angle. If not anything, these are poems written, read and edited more than usually; there is more writing, more reading and more editing before it comes to the reader. There are more consciousnesses than one at work in many of these pieces. These collaborative efforts have led to abstruse relations of mutual construction as well as deconstruction of the authorial 'self' and 'authority'. It has involved acknowledging the other as well as negotiating differences—a collaborative creativity and a creative collaboration. There has been a dispersal of author/ity—not a juxtaposition of individually created pieces, but a sharing of textual spaces. It would have been possible for us to segregate these poems individually. It would be possible for you as a reader to segregate them as each author's. But we deem this segratory activity redundant, since reading the lived reality of one person on to the poems he or she writes is an inane and largely unrewarding enterprise.

Arun & Sunitha

CONTENTS

COMPRENDRE

I
Come, comprehend Love
in wakeful hours
like how we comprehend
the foggy winding road
on a night drive
by the flooding headlight.

II
Come, comprehend Life
like a yellow bird
sitting warm on its eggs
comprehends miracles
happening beneath her belly.

III
Come, comprehend Decay
like a shifting flame comprehends
the melting of a candle into
wax and grime.

IV

Come, comprehend Death
from a tumbled steel glass that runs to the table's edge,
slowly stops and stares at us with its vacant mouth

V

Come, comprehend Eternity
like how the columns of a golden dusk that shine on a lake
give way
and it is night again
and poems surface from the mute depth.

LOTUS ISLAND

The misty mountain melts a moon in its hair.
The wind whispers through the ears of wild lily.
Within the grove, slow shadows move.
The air holds incense in its heart.

Your ship is still asleep:
Above the mast clouds lock fingers.
Somewhere on the island,
A large mirror gathers vapour waiting for your face.

A WHILE AFTER

A while after you left the table
I noticed your words scalded
At the broken mouth
Of the teacup

THE LOST ARMY

In the hour of the wolf
The tide threw up cadavers --
Limbs ribs entrails uniforms insignias --
Onto a moonlit beach:
Bones tacked on the glistening sand.
Loose skins, like leather pouches,
Held brine and bullets.
Wave after wave pulled them back
To the tide-mouth.
Their silent howls climbed the vault of the universe.

The nighthawk descended,
Burst open with its promethean beak
The lost army's sore past:
Like dark blood,
A poem
Now spreads through the sand.

"In the Hour of the Wolf" *The Criterion: An International Journal of English,* Vol7, issue3, june2016 ISSN-0976-8165

HIS NAME WAS NANU

His name was Nanu.
He was the last public madman of our village.
He raided the temple coconut-groves at night
And slept naked by the mosque's viscous-green pond during day.

Maybe because he loved the pond more,
He changed his faith,
Became Mammu
And lived another couple years
Before dying in the temple's coconut grove on a rainy night.

Only the mad
And this poem
Will remember him.

MASK

A mask hides the mouth –
It is a drill for the eyes
In smiling, scorning, scandalising.

A mask hides the hook of the nose -
It allows only a crooked breath.

A mask is a prayer –
May this infected air lift,
May we soon put this covering where it came from –
May we wear it across our hearts once again.

LEECHES

Inching towards the warmth,
Tugging and feeling real,
Sucking and draining
Off deep gory gashes
Ever raw and pulsing,
Sinking deep in silken deceit,
Leaving stingers, lumps, and shards
A shard-sharp tongue of flame licking on the skin,
Sticking holes in the night beneath the pain -
Tiny holes that shine like stars silver and reticent.
Leeching: deep, to the heart's content.

BROKEN HINGES

Life on hinges broken
Creaking rusted
Hanging heavy
Closing on bodies rotten burrowed
Slimy slithery dismembering vengeance
Stinking wormy gaping gashes
Slurping and feasting maggots
An inching huddled shroud.

METAPHORS FOR SILENCE IN LOVE

Silence in love
is a dull wall
where sunlight makes and unmakes
semblances of the lover's face all through the day.

Silence in love
is a grey curtain
that hangs heavy
indifferent to the breezing life

Silence in love
is a stillborn poem,
cold and blue, in the brain.

Silence in love
is black slithery fanged coil
hidden in the damp grass
waiting for your feet
to draw closer.

WHEN YOU HOLD THE HAND OF A LITTLE GIRL

When you hold the hand of a little girl
as she plays in the evening sea,
you let your complexities and secrets
flow into the surf
that tricks away
the ground beneath your feet,

and you become the blunt emotion of
a stem that holds a tender leaf back
from flying loose in a storm.

You feel your grip pulse
as the sun dissolves in the sea where she plays,
as your clothes gather wet clutches of sand,
as the briny wind dries in your hair.

The sea tumbles at the hem of her skirt
and breaks in foam after blissful foam on the shore:
Her hand glows through the pinprick gaps in your fist.
Like a herb that bore a shining fruit,
you develop a strange aura on the darkening beach.

When you hold the hand of a little girl
as she plays in the sea,
you understand,
vaguely,
why the living heart is like a fist,
clutching and easing, and never letting go.

INTO A CITY OF DISQUIET

Into a city of disquiet I set out
Every morning, dark and foreboding,
Sailing through waves deadly
With a chalice of black venom
Hissing and spewing a murderous potion
To pierce with a whetted sword
To suspend in a hanging noose
Thoughts swift trampling horses racing

THESEUS

The mouth of the maze was skewed in reproof
As I tugged at my spool of perfumed thread;
A word moved in my throat its steely hoof;
A neighing dread across my thoughts was spread.
Beyond the mountain caps the motley dawn
In sacrificial clouds of scarlet hue
Combed leafy trees with windy fingers drawn
And redrawn in unusual ado.

Bear me in your songs, Ariadne,
And ferry me over the Minotaur's
Labyrinth of blood, to my destiny
Where valour and desire in due course
Melt in half-truths of dreams and golden myths.
It becomes of the king to wish my death:
Sloth numbing his vengeful head's laurel wreaths,
Incensed pride sputtering in his breath.

I shall not share the ignominy of
My predecessors – I have your ball of thread.
I sense moments undoing Fate's handcuff –
It's now that I should move my mortal tread.

The beast is hidden somewhere far inside;
Its deed but vaporizing in foul-clouds
Cling on every bristly bush that guide
Or misguide me who grope his way through clods.
Ah! Why must your love's yarn snap so soon?
Why, Why should these trees close in on the track
Like night closes its thighs around the moon
And stands up glistening on a low shack!
I see the horizons have come undone.
There is no salvation – no after-life –
It's ending Ariadne; as the wind
Howls, I half-sense your dark mouth me engulf.

"Theseus" *The Criterion: An International Journal of English*, Vol7, issue3, june2016 ISSN-0976-8165

PENSIVE NOTES

Words and lines piled on each other
Gliding stanzas slip one into the other
Little eyes skim and scan
Toppling into pensive notes
Burying you in a stillness that hoots

METAPHORS FOR DEATH

Death is a rotting body in the yard
Light shining on its wet skull
now that the skin is left to the ants
And flesh to the vengeance of worms.

Death is a body beneath the sunny grass
Indifferent to the roots that gash
and carry the rot to leaves and buds.

AT TIMES

At times
Heart feels like a sprawling cemetery

So many people lie buried
Under stones carrying names and dates.

O at night, when a ghost howls,
Among the windswept trees,
Or when a withered flower
Ends itself in the afternoon,
Or when a forlorn man, woman, or child walks past
Silent and heavy with memories,
The heart feels like an old sprawling cemetery.

COMMUTER REVISITED

The commuter
Tapping on a luminous glare
Dozes off to earplugged music
Blind to
Clouds spread cotton puffs
Up above
the bus in a bright blue sky.
Below,
the road runs
A shooting leopard
Leaving behind slow walls stationary
waking dogs and shop-shutters.

WORDS

Words are likes dislikes thoughts wishes desires
Words are you and me

Yet, a word is also a world
Turned empty
As it spurts cold pebbles on me

Pebbles that bounce
And scatter around me
Mocking the beings
Of likes dislikes thoughts wishes desires
Mine
A world of forgotten words, Yours.

THE DAY IS NOT YET DONE...

The day is not yet done:
It is walking the road to the night
Lit by the moon.
Clasping each other's dear hands
We hold our woes in silence
As it soars into the night
And escapes our sight.

THE PIG WHO LEARNT TO FLY

The Pig who Learnt to Fly
Flew up and high
Towards the sky.

A pig
From the butcher's,
Groaning and grunting
Sniffing and snorting
Pestered by the slaughterhouse
Flew up and high.

A pig
Amongst a somnolent circus crowd
Pout-faced twisting ears
Tugging at his rope
Squealing squirming and wriggling
Flew up and high.

Until
Feet in the air he took off
From the poke and the prod
Giggling at the gesticulating knife.

Down below,
As its bulging flesh
Burst at the seams,
Away he flew from the pigsty,
The pig who learnt to fly.

AND SHE GREW UP...

A day like any
The morning hustle
Children a-bustle
The sun in boredom
Glaring in routine
The wind as ever
Flipping through lives

A day like any
Until a minuscule world
Was toppled in convulsions
And through many lives
A seizure passed

Hearts burned
As needles pricked
A skin soft calm
And medicines spread
Through veins in balm
Eyes opened to life anew
And tremulous stirred a body unsound
Unsure of the world around

A day like any
Was painted white
With peering faces
In search of respite
A home anxious lost in thought
Seeking refuge in what was lost.

ICY MIRROR

The icy mirror misty calm
A duple rainbow chimeral flow
Pylons and bridges cutting through
A hazy white
Snuggling cosy in its cradle below

CUPID I THOUGHT WAS LOVE...

Cupid I thought was love
His arrow, a seed sprouting.

Valentine I thought was love
His blessings a shower
That beaded together many.

Love I thought was life
At an altar crucified
Echoing painfully in many.

Love I thought was the many
Gifts cards hands and eyes
Together held unknotted

Love I thought was in You
A world without adieu
Fading to residue
As felt in my sinew
Pulsating every moment anew
Love I thought I knew
Until
I met Love
And Love met me

MY SEARCH

My search for the source of this river
Full, even in bone-wracking summer,
Tossing boats, drowning boatmen,
Dirty red, warm-rippled, torn, loud,

Ended in your eyes.

A STONY SILENCE

Throwing life
A voice directionless
Reverberating
A stony silence of words
Here comes the ventriloquist!
Talking to his self invisible
A puppet and a puppeteer
Fading into each other

I

I Savitri, the ideal wife
Of whom the sage Markandeya spoke
A curse to the world

I Sita
Of whom Valmiki wrote
Consort of Rama, a Paragon of virtues
Onerous to the world

Now I am Kali
The slayer of Raktabija
Garlanded with death
The Goddess of the dark
Yet I
Shiva Shakti.

HEELS OF GREATNESS

To be invincible with a vulnerable spot
Alcides, as your mother dipped you in Styx
Her fingers on your soles tightly held
Riveted like Oedipus, you shivered at your fate
To be distraught at the loss of an armour to Hector
As Hephastos forged the shield of Achilles
And inspired ages many
The vain attempt to save a son
As Paris' arrow Apollo steered
Seared the vulnerable heels of greatness

A FULLMOON NIGHT

From the shadowy tree
A white bird flapped its large wings
And flew away.

Naked and spent
We watched it
Through the bedroom window.

THE DARK

Agile leeward moves
The gradient javelin
Delirious, quivering sharp
Piercing the blanket of night

LITTLE HEARTS

Teeny-weeny beads around
Tiny tots here abound

Romping kids sit and smile
Innocent of every vile

Tiny kittens paw and roll
Mewing, purring over a ball

Ships many set a sail
Onward searching Holy Grail

Blinking eyelids fade asleep
Into a world of nightmare weep
Winking stars sparkle high
As little hearts burst in sigh

THE FAERIE TALE

Mirror mirror on the wall
Who is the fairest of them all

From inside the silvery cloud
Emerged a carpet of magic

A cornucopia of memories phoney
Fluttered like curtains

In peered Snow White's apple
and Red Riding's grandma in hoods

Into the house of seven dwarfs
In a forest of grizzly bears

Clock strikes twelve like a whiplash
And a head rattles of fatigue.

SIGHTSEEING IN THE CAPITAL

A Land of the Dead
Embalmed in tombs
Preserved in Red Forts.
Death dogging every itinerant step:
Rajghat or Gateway.
A museum of visitors.

A BELCHING SILENCE

Of,
Starved rats, empty houses and tiles fallen
People stuffing themselves with filth
Eyeing each other suspiciously
Waiting like cats for scraps
Amidst stench of sewers and power lines
Snails crunchily squashed to paste
Puffing vehicles hurrying with animal sounds
Wailing babies and pliable streets
Drooping cigarettes
Stinking washrooms
Vain shouts, imprecations inexhaustible.

Somewhere a bored man behind the bar
Levers himself away to a bottle
Slow and sluggish moves…n slams the bottle down now
That asshole in Nike!
"Worms!" he spits out
"I'll blow you to pieces"
His gaze around….
BLAAM!
(Oh! Cut it out for God's sake)

Like mad dogs tearing to bits
Dreaming of neighbour's wife
Blown over rusty lives that tumble down like sheds
Hoarse voices, gaping shitpots
Flushing out filthy larvae
Maggots crawling up skirts

To hell with the world!!
A silence that belches emptiness

SOME DAYS

Some days are like stray dogs:
They won't cease till they drag the worst
Out of what's been piling up in the dumping yard.

OUT ON A DRIVE

I left my house and drove past
Moving people, buildings, houses, trees and cars
My mind too glided
Swiftly past the scenes
Never static in search
Of the faces pushed behind,
One after another
A sudden break before the traffic lights red
That paused all around
The fish seller with his crows and cats lazing around
The chicken stall with its clacking hens and dirty floor
The vegetable vendor green-red, yellow-orange inviting
People hurrying at zebra crossings
Ducking vehicles refusing way
A bumpy ride through the roads winding
The rider up-down-here-n there
And back to his life.

NUT HOUSE

Could you tell me if the earth is moving
This stubborn stench of putrefaction prognosticates doom
Climbing down your face, down your belly
In this dark private coffin
My heart beating like a kitten's
A bulging fleshed coffin
Amede! Absurd these rumblings
Hoa! Rotting life, its gaping closets
Nothing happens, only stagnant rot
Stars falling, here! I caught one
In my fists lest it melt
The silver shines and oozes out between my fingers
And dewdrops appear on leaves
Yeah, you are right
I just ran away from the nuthouse
They are searching for me, the prowling fugitive.

A MEMORIAL

This wall against which I write and live
A board black and blank
Words creep on and off it
As lives appear and disappear
Cracks and fissures appear
Bricks dislodged, loose
The wall remains
A memorial
Of a life
Mine.

FIN

I sit amidst ruins
In throes of doubt
Unable to write
A life apart at the seams
Charred words
A black muck
Strewn around amidst a
Rising sun of gold
Clinging to rotten memories
in a well-kept prison
My own private darkness
Prodding me on to the end
End of everything
End of the world.

THE MUNDANE

Pulled out
Dragged into a miserable life
Of cigarette butts
Scratching bellies and bobbing tits
Elephantine thighs sighing
Monotonous piddling arses
Faecal couches mating worms
I surface into a sweet coolness
Amidst an array of stray cats
Clutching my bag as it slapped against my side

A CLOUD CANDY

Clouds that move and not
Grey dusky black
Enveloping darkness
Fighting against a tide that
Sails above meditative mirrors
Clears only to gather
A pace its own

To look up and not find
The sky above!
Left tiny on a vacuous space!
Like smoke that chokes
Like cotton candies that whirl around
Floating yet never disappearing
Emerging a cloud candy flossed
To be held between fingers

TAPESTRY

Women
Imprisoned in Thrace
Weaving into tapestry
A muted fate and crime
Of brute Tereus
Proclaiming to the world a base deed

A woman violated another incensed
To a cannibal meal of ire
That transformed
into a swallow and a nightingale

Lives that flew through ages
Of existence violated
Swooping into each
As partakers of crime.

DELIRIUM

Glistening blue
Lost in shadowy hue
Helter skelter spectre talk
Frozen patches ghastly walk
Delirious galley stirred
Agony of death deferred

HE WALKS THE EARTH

To hilt phoney
Fleeced to bone
Thumping clanging
Cracks and fissures unsealed
Bone dry
He walks the earth
As swooping intolerance pillage and massacre

FAITH

Ground by worms
Postulant sealed
An unpredictable monster
Faith
A sore thumb

LEGACY

Towering icicle resolute
Suffering votaries corpulent
Delusive sanctity
Religious verbiage
Intricate cruelty
Abandoned heritage
Derisive Indian absolute
Heroic legacy opulent

US

My roots go deep inside you.
Your warmth feeds my fruition,
Your silence, my leafless season.

And when I try to pull away from you
It tugs and tears your flesh in a thousand ways:
We can't die but in a pair, in mutual disgrace.

DAGGER WORDS

Your dagger words dart through darkness
Clang in my head
Rattle as grinding attacks
On (what you call) my burgeoning intelligence.

A slanderous blob of phlegm
A grimace (my reply) that takes
A life time to compose
And settle as saccharine illusions.

PHANTOM THOUGHTS

In your monotonous existence
I dog every step
Offering a choice between two
Amidst the fan churning laboriously
In a vacant air
Amidst a stultifying life of yours
Tormented by the clock
And a fan wearing itself out

I lurk in ambush behind every step of yours
Amidst rooms filled with monotonous silence
And turgid pavements
Bogged by phantoms
Dangling precarious amidst putrid love
Yet you with a head balanced
On shoulders — bobbing and bumping
Not stumbling
Spilling...

A BOUQUET

A forbidden cupboard of memories grotesque
A freezing metal welling from the pores
Burning holes searching for concealed fangs
Crumpled ripples
Wrinkled fatigue
Corroded brain
A heirloom
A bouquet of dry roses
Lie scattered like red blebs of life

THE GODDESS

She opened her eyes and said,
Why do these obeisant multitudes come to me for favours?
So many!
I'm tired...
Listening day and night to all your fawning deceit
To all the hollow promises you make to see yourself blessed
Goddesses too get tired, you know
For god'sake (ha !) leave me alone for a while
Goddesses too need to be alone
To recuperate
Before inane wishes are granted
To keep Her idol revered.

THE PANDEMIC

Nations fall, one after the other,
Like it was all a house of cards,
Falling, as people breathe violet into the maps,
Falling so fast -
This moment's peace could be my last.
Literature falls in no time at all,
Theories fall,
Hoardings and highways and hospitals fall,
Unto dust collapses the classroom wall.

They fall, they fall inside your head,
Trailing curses that escaped
The clogged lungs of the lately dead.

You fumble on behalf of the living,
But it cuts you short and dictates what is right
In a way only a microbe can:
It neither lived nor died,
Nor desired nor lost,
Never waged a war, never fought in one,
It has only evolved, only multiplied to further evolve.
Death is as good as Life

To this windy indifference.
The Beginning is as good as the End
To this slow-burning omnipresence.
You want to rein in the contagion, but it shocks you
Destroying tomorrow all that was gained today.
A fall gains, and it gains so fast
Zero to sixty in no time gets passed.
They can't make enough coffins for the dead;

They can't dig enough graves for the coffined:
Continents bloat with confessions unsaid,
Sea winds mop with blue-fog the dreams unmade.

You don't fight the police anymore;
There are no fiery slogans anymore;
No firing order; no flying fists.
It's useless to fight History with News;

Your brains tick, tick so fast
This moment's peace could be your last;
Better crouch and hide away like the lesser beast.

Online campaigns rumble away over your hideouts;
They prop falling nations against
Pulp-printed instruction-boards
And display atop your quarantine
A film-star's hope-cast
Every fifteen minutes.
Tables have turned,
The blue mist brings cracked faces
To the windows of conscience:
They have pale marbles where there were eyes before.
Far off somewhere, sirens blast;
This moment's peace could be the last.

I IPHIGENIA

Let the ships sail to Troy with me
For Calchas, I Iphigenia at the altar stand
(or am I princess Eriphile)
Before Artemis and a wailing Tyndareus' daughter
At Aulis a woman laid down her life
Like the many to quell the gales
For the troops to sail and a mother
To wreak vengeance for Tantalus and me
To share an unholy bed with
Agamemnon and Aegisthus
Deceived of life and Aegisthus
An unaware Achilles to marry

I willingly sacrificed
To be whisked away
To the priestess of Artemis
To escape with Orestes to Argive
To be worshipped in Heroic Age
By Euripides at Aulis and in Tauris
To Aulis not for Achilles
But Artemian altar
To Tauris and return with Orestes

The avenger of Agamemnon
Borne to Zminthe and Chryses
Hellenic goddess of wilderness
O Artemis

I stand alone on the shores
A woman
A fate sacrificed
A marvellous spectacle of ships
A formidable Armada
I look and stand by a land of deceit
I stand below the same skies
By a daughter's murderer
A madman

The King of Hellenes
Must I pay the penalty for your mistakes
You shall not slay your child
Who is to be my groom?
Order the hymeneals to echo
Peleus' son, Achilles, a name to snare the halls
How shall you receive me?
You before Priams' Paris with Helen's hand
By Atreus that begot us
I pity you
I your ruin
Before the Achean host with Calchas Oracles
Unable to flee to Argos
The city razed to ground
The dower gifts sacrificial
Turn in dismay
A heavy burden laid on me
by the Phrygian city and Helen
The lustural waters ready

Come Iphiginia obedient to a father's purpose
A tale of woes
To be seized by force from the son of Thyestes
Yet defended by Tyndareus to bear you fruits
Now kill daughter that Menelaus may have Helen
For Hellas that you offer me as sacrifice
Let the rites be initiated
Let the fire blaze
Let the Oracle circle the altar
For I bring Hellenes salvation and victory
Sing the praise of Artemis

A knife out of the scabbard drew
The priest grasped and prayed
Seeking where to strike
And lo behold! the maiden vanished
Orestes avenged the blood of my father
By slaying my mother
And to the Tauric land with Pylades for the goddess' image
I dwell apart far from those who think me cruelly slaughtered
A life cursed that bewails him that is dead in Argos
The infant Orestes i left
Make ready the rites of consecration
For two strangers form Hellene
To know of my land my people

Sued by Artemis made priestess
Orestes to retrieve image of Artemis
I brought to Aulis by treachery
Tell me of Oretses Helen, Calchas
Achilles and Agamemnon, accursed Tantalid
Fetch me back to Argos before i die
And Thoas to Athena's words subdues
I seek my land.

FORGIVE ME

Forgive me if my words hurt you,

Like a head teacher in her office forgives the parent
Whose children broke the classroom window:

Forgive my words for breaking your clear window.

TROOTH ACHE

They check the horse's teeth to see if it's worth,
They check the cow's teeth,
And what's a dog minus its canines!

That's why I think teeth hold more
Truths than what meets the eye:
A squeaky shiny smile might have rotten inner truths.
A blank smile may have strong back-stories.

Sometimes from the mouth of people
Dead ones smile. Dead teeth bite on living fruits.
Dead teeth chatter in living fears.

And sometimes, I think, a skull is just a dead excuse
To mount a living full-toothed grin.

THANK GOD

Thank God I have a fickle heart,
Or I would never understand why betrayal
Is just the price we pay for desire.

RIVER SUTRA

Every river leaps from the Earth's loins
And runs
Down green hills
And busy towns
And dark forests
Through mud
And mouldy rocks
Rolling stones
And tossing fish

Till

The sea
Will teach it
The secret salt of tears
And the need to slow down and sigh.

DREAMSCAPE

I walk into the clouds
For a hand to hold
A hand firm and fast
Holding me to myself

Into the smoke I lose myself
As bits and pieces chip and fall
I find myself amidst shadows of death
Each gasping for life
In a hell one's own
Amidst a cauldron of seething questions
A blessing the moist lips on my forehead
The only reality bearable

Darkness descends with a sickle sharp
That scrapes and scathes my being

SKY AND SEA

And one day, the sea made love to the sky:
The birds raided the blue deep
And swam up with coral on their wings;
The fish grazed the meteors
And flew down with stardust in their scales.
One day, after aeons of waiting, the sea and the sky made love:
A million stars exploded in the waves;
The moon slithered through the baptizing fluid.

And, the sky made love to the sea.
Vermillion and purple burst through the tides,
Salt sprayed through rainbows.

And when they slept, spent,
The fish went about nosing the stars.
And a white trail of clouds floated on the waters.

OF A COUPLE WHO GROW OLD TOGETHER

The life of that old couple
Followed the pace and soft shapes
Of large clouds in late summer:
Not moving, only shifting
In each other's dissolving certainties.

And one held out only as long as
The other was still afloat.

YOUR NAME..

I'll never write an autobiography
For fear of waking up your name
That now is resting in the heart

Like a hornet nested on a library wall.

BEING IN LOVE

Being in love
Is being born again:
Being in a womb Afloat Eyes shut Nibbling air
Listening to the world outside like it's a distant whisper
Growing new organs Getting bigger and Bigger

Till one day
You're pushed and shoved and squeezed
Through blood and tear and filth
And you cry and cry and cry your way out.

SKELETAL VERSE

I toss and turn unable to contain
the river in spate gushing forth
A fear too
of all that it will take along
Of all that will cling to me
like drained silt
The banks dry
like skeletons shorn

ART ACQUIRED

I have learnt to smile
Yes, smile...smile…smile
Learnt to smile
I learnt that to smile it takes a lot of effort
I learnt to make that effort
The effort
To smile when i don't feel like
To smile when it hurts
To smile when i hate
To smile as my drained cheeks tremble
To smile as my pricking eyes drizzle
To smile as my stinging heart burns
To smile for others
It takes more effort...
More effort than learning
alphabets
numbers
languages
the ways of life
...all
Yes, i have learnt the greatest lesson
Of distorting and disfiguring myself
The toughest chapter in the book of life.

YOU AND I

A clink!
Shattered webs
And a s p l i n t e r
Each shard
further smashed to smithereens
Scattered red petals
Amidst crunching footsteps
Dying into the dark.

I your eyes
To live, to smile, to burn, to flood n drown...
Your eyes I

A WORLD THAT IS NOT MINE

Every night I say Goodnight
To a world that is not mine

Every night I say Goodnight
To a world that disappears into the dark...

Every night a Goodnight
Seals my day tight

Every night a Goodnight
Wakes me to my doom.

DON'T DO

Do not seek the poet in the poem
For it takes more than his menagerie,
Memory, skill, skull, luck, love, felicity
Or even the poem itself –
To write a poem.

LOVE IS A NIGHT ANIMAL

Love is a night animal that raids ripe fields:
The books say it'd be caught and put in a cage;
But usually, in full moons, it's simply shot dead.

DRIED-UP RIVERS AREN'T RIVERS

Dried-up rivers aren't rivers.
The hollow might carry the name of the river,
The wind over the sand might occasionally smell of fish,
The bridge that crosses it might have water weeds on the pillars,

But like love that ended would the lights of love abhor
A river that dries is not a river anymore.

MY WINE

My wine is bitter
I'll down it like medicine.
My songs are harsh
I'll with them break my curses.

My love is a storm
O, I'll take it like wet grass.

BODIES AFTER LOVE

Bodies after love
Are like emptied wine bottles:
Despite the clarity of the glass,
Despite the lightness,
There's this sad sad smell of a red potion that refuses to leave.

EVERY RIVER

Every river flows
As trees on the bank look on,
Unblinking.

Every bird flies
As clouds slowly disperse
Above them.

Every lover burns
As clocks coldly breathe
Down their time.

THERE'S A WINDOW

There's a broken window
That I've kept unrepaired.

When a day looks very clear and sunny
And everything's so calm and birds and butterflies

I shift to that window and regain my vision.

SARASWATHI

Of the woman's two breasts, one is Music:
Comprehension itself is pleasure.

The other is poetry: comprehension
Precedes contemplation, and the pleasure,
Often long-winded, if not elusive.

No wonder children obsess on them
As do lovers.

A SLIT IN THE SKY

Look! A slit in the flaming sky
Hidden cotton candies bulging
Here 'n there
A burning lozenge on a marble shroud
Slowly doused on the skyline
Into blinking stars lopsided
A looped moon chasing darkness into corners
O! Celestial sphere
What madness!!

LOVE

Our bodies move in the fever of love:
Why should you suddenly throw a sidelong glance
At the lone goldfish in the bowl?

SHE WAS CRYING

She was crying aloud
And I was thinking
It sounded like tearing paper
Tearing it lengthwise, tearing paper
That carried poetry, tearing it, tearing it.

THE PARABLE OF THE SPARROW AND THE SPRING

I was the sparrow destined to call out
The spring that slept inside you.

Now,
Sitting on a branch drenched in bursting beauty
The startled sparrow listens to the voicing wild.

NOBODY WAS PERFECT

Nobody was perfect:
I wanted to be Nobody.

But then,
As I grew up,
One summer afternoon
Nobody saw me standing alone
At the busy streetside.

Nobody said I was perfect
And came running to me
Wanting to be me.

FREEDOM

Freedom is the path of a bullet
That has left the barrel
But not hit the flesh
Yet.

LIKE BLOOD

Like blood gushing
out of a man shot in the chest
lying face down
dying on a deserted night-street,
a dark poem streams through my brain.

CONTRARY TO LOVE

He thought of love as a rain;
She knew love to be what the rain leaves
On leaf-tips, on grass-blades and in swift
Streams that'll eventually clog, puddle up and stink,
Before it dies.

NATIONAL HERITAGE

Under a tropical sun's voyeur eye,
Your ripe body quakes in intervals,
Erupts in bloody irregular riots,
Floods in bouts,
And tries quickbites of frosty fanaticism.

Open-armed
Cross-thighed
You, my mermaid-nation!

MEMORY IS A PICKLE JAR

Memory is a pickle jar
Where we deposit our days, evenly sliced:

Every time we feast someone with our stories,
We shake the jar, and pick from the preservative,
Those slices that have shrivelled well
And have lost enough of what was real.

JUST LIKE THAT

Just like that
My poem ran into the rain
Took off all its words
And started dancing.

THE SEA THIS EVENING

The sea this evening
Is a grey disease
Foaming at the mouth.

PHONETIKISS

Some kisses stop at bilabial plosives,
Some advance to labiodentals,
While some dare the velar extents.

But think of those kisses
That foreclose all sounds
And investigate silence.

LOVE AND OTHER SINS

Like Sin
Love affects only those
Who believe.

Like Sin
Love makes its committing subject
Dearer to Providence.

Like Sin
Love cleaves and scars,
Weighs and deepens.

Like Sin, O like Sin
Love breeds poems from free speech
And makes grown ups of sprightly children.

LIFE

Paths that twine and entwine
Into the infinite sunny depths
Latticed with misty dark and frost
A hesitant hand reaches out
But slithers thither in fear

A RUSTLING LEAF

Walking through life
A leaf rustling in the wind
A wafting skeletal veil
That hugs the earth

LUST AND LOVE

Lust is a Fog.
Love, the diffused light
Breaking with difficulty through the fog,
Calling the traveller,
Calling him to the other side.

GYPSIES

Into the one-horse town of my head
On every low-moon night
Like gypsy carnivals
Your dreams arrive.

BOREDOM

Once boredom catches on it just doesn't stop:
Boredom is interested in statistics,
Boredom is interested in sex,
Boredom is interested in cinema, books, and booze,
Boredom is interested in enemies, friends and news.

Boredom is bored about practically nothing:
Such vigour!

YEARTIDE—AN INDIAN POEM

Rebellious ringlets tucked behind her ears
A child holding his fingers tight
I walked your shores
Grains of sand slipping
Through my fingers little
A witness to life, mine and yours

I tried rebuilding castles
Washed away on your shores
Your cold silver reflecting my life
As gliding vessels, constantly on move
As peanut vendors and ballooned hawkers
Bottled colours and crowded shores
Echoed in my eyes and ears

I romped on your shores
Waves kissing my growing feet
Drenched in love and hate
Blissful and unaware
Your waves echoed a music
Heavy and lashing calm

Young I walked your tiled shores
Happy by you glistening in the sun
Life receding like you
As I whisked past in happiness
You shared my heaviness and silence
My love, sorrow and disappointments
Even letting those flooding tears of mine
Merge in your salty silent depths
As I stood on your shores then
And now my fingers curling desperately
Into your sheet of death
Reminding me of the moment my life parted from yours...

TIME

Fleeting golden hues
Fading grains of sand
Tick tock the clock
Wrapped in calm embrace
A flash and a blink
And life passes by
I try to make it slow
I try to make it pause
Just to make us live
The hourglass strains itself
Tides rock my boat
My memories tell me so
Wish I could fade
The clock in my room has stopped
I fall a little deeper
Lost the fear of losing
Myself
A fevered dream
And all comes to end.

A RENT

And Life passes by
Eyes grazing the landscape
Yearning for visions blissful
Amidst those leaving and left behind
And slipping words haywire
Renting love and faith
Life passes by....

DUMB WORDS

Words dumb
Talk with us
Turn cold with us
One day I met them on my way
Traipsing and tromping on theirs
I told them how they had changed!
They looked at me questioningly
I blinked and smiled
You have changed...changed said i
...from the helpmate you were
to a slut who struts fore all..
...of each and every now
...a zilch..
.. .mine, yet never...
Words smirked, and said...
We like being posted into an empty space
Waiting with bated breath for likes
Words unreliable, said my mind in disdain
(written for You…with warmth-
A hope that meets its definite end)
And Words replied,
We wait for likes...wait to be flaunted

Your surfeit eyes bent, look for Likes
not us...Words
Unfaithful words! said I
nailed to me
oozing off me
As I bear the burden writhing in pain...

A CREASED REFLECTION

Birds high among the stars
Houses scattered quiet and calm
Braided river gazing cold
A creased reflection of the morn

Clouds of peace soon ripped apart
Agents of chaos pulling strings
Aged cadavers from the past
A game perfect with foolish pawns
Rodents gnawing in the black
Furious fingers slicing air
Shadows tremble in the dark
Smelling of human animals wild
Into a night of our making own
Cover my eyes!

LETTERS OF LOVE

Letter from a Daughter...
(please spare Madame Elektra)

Dear...,
I have survived!
I write this to tell you what I cannot now
To thank you for placing me in your life as a daughter
In your sons' as a sister, loved and cared
For always telling me in your own way
That you were blessed to have me (the fierce and stubborn me) in your life
Thank you I needn't...I know it...
For holding my hands when I faltered
For filling me with the poise of being a woman
As I wrestled with the Waves
For letting me take my own decisions and stand by them
For equipping me to grapple with life, its whirlwinds
For silently teaching me all through my life
To face this moment...
For putting these words into me
For making my life free of the volley of 'ifs n buts'
For asking me to breathe freely
Unchained by malicious daggers sharp and blunt

For making me realize the beauty of soaring high and far
With my wings unsinged
For keeping my feet firm on the ground,
Shoulders high and eyes sparkling
For teaching me a woman is a woman
Pride, care, Love and Life
A liberated sovereign ferocious
Reason and Heart

And you knew I would
Survive…

Love you…

LIKE AN ANIMAL

Like an animal
My poem waits at your doorstep:

It cannot understand your doubts;
It does not understand your thoughts:

Like an animal it keeps its senses alert
For the moment you'll stop thinking
And receive its helpless love.

JOURNEY

Choosing to tread the road of love
Is to forego the joy of broad and pleasant highways
for a forest trail that lets little light in,
and gives scant sense of direction.

You're on a path where Ancients have walked
But there are no footprints to lead:
You feel like you began this path
And it's bound to end with you.

ALREADY

I leave a poem in the top left hand side of the page
And exit through the bottom right hand corner.

Already the poem is turning to white dust;
Black ants are carrying the sweeter bits to the top right hand side:
Maybe that's where the ants live.

Already the day is leaving the calendar of my future
With notes from my poem in its coat-pocket.
Already Memory has started stalking the day.
At some deserted corner, with a swinging hammer,
The day will be put to an end
And its body thrown in a dark ditch.

From the dead day's pocket,
Notes of my poem will fall off and wait
For a remote ray of sun to arrive some day, some remote day.